A Crabtree Branches Book

Improving Your Social Skills

TELLING THE TRUTH

VICKY BUREAU

Crabtree Publishing
crabtreebooks.com

School-to-Home Support for Caregivers and Teachers

This high-interest book is designed to motivate striving students with engaging topics while building fluency, vocabulary, and an interest in reading. Here are a few questions and activities to help the reader build upon his or her comprehension skills.

Before Reading:

- *What do I think this book is about?*
- *What do I know about this topic?*
- *What do I want to learn about this topic?*
- *Why am I reading this book?*

During Reading:

- *I wonder why...*
- *I'm curious to know...*
- *How is this like something I already know?*
- *What have I learned so far?*

After Reading:

- *What was the author trying to teach me?*
- *What are some details?*
- *How did the photographs and captions help me understand more?*
- *Read the book again and look for the vocabulary words.*
- *What questions do I still have?*

Extension Activities:

- *What was your favorite part of the book? Write a paragraph on it.*
- *Draw a picture of your favorite thing you learned from the book.*

TABLE OF CONTENTS

What Is the Truth? 4

Why the Truth Is So Important 6

Honesty vs Dishonesty 8

Checkpoint: What Would You Do? 10

Why Do We Lie? 12

Emotions and Lying 14

Understanding Integrity 16

Understanding Responsibility 18

Checkpoint: What Would You Do? 20

Understanding Accountability 23

How to Fix a Lie 25

Learning to Be Honest 27

A Better You 29

Glossary 30

Index 31

Websites to Visit 31

About the Author 32

WHAT IS THE TRUTH?

Do you always tell the **truth**?

To tell the truth means you are saying something that agrees with facts or reality. Think about books, like the one you are reading now. This book is nonfiction, which means that it is about facts that are not made up. It tells what is true. It is different from a fiction book, which is a made-up story.

WHY THE TRUTH IS SO IMPORTANT

You may wonder why telling the truth is so important.

Telling the truth is important because it helps to show that you are an **honest** person. When you are honest with people, it shows them that they can trust you and the things that you say. More so, when you tell the truth, you show **integrity**, **responsibility**, and **accountability**.

DID YOU KNOW?

Honesty increases our connection with others and our **self-esteem**.

HONESTY VS DISHONESTY

Let's explore the difference between honesty and dishonesty.

Remember, being honest means that you are telling the truth. The truth means that what you are saying agrees with facts or reality. On a clear, sunny day, you would be telling the truth in saying that it is not raining.

Being dishonest means you purposely say something that you know is not true. On a clear, sunny day, you would be dishonest by saying that it is raining, even though you are dry and can feel the warm sun!

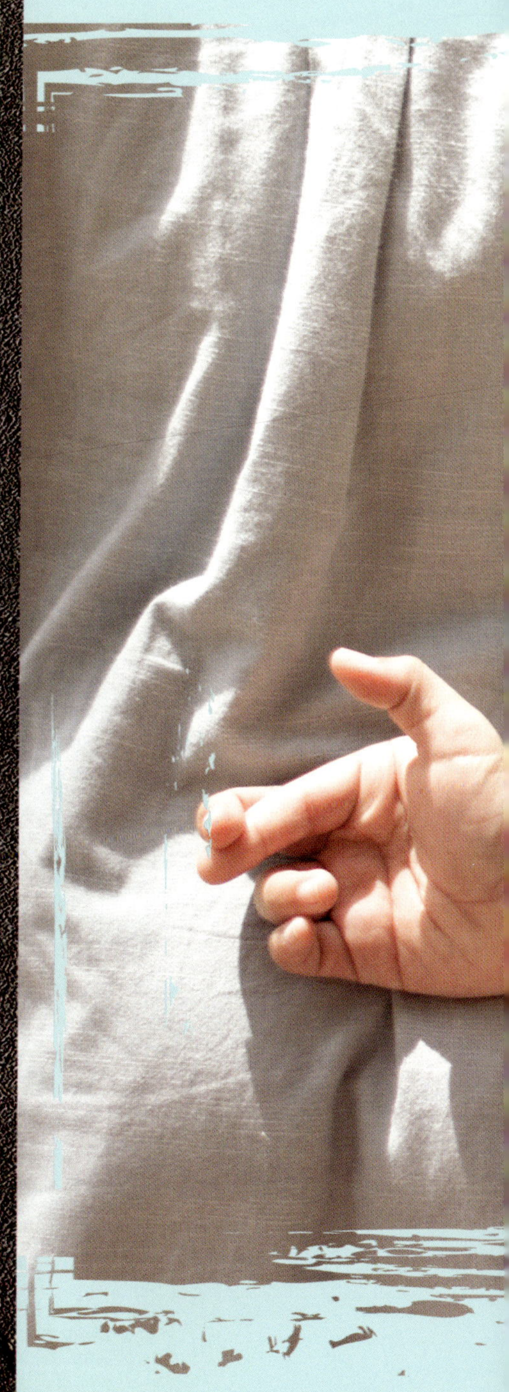

DID YOU KNOW?

One of the most common reasons for dishonesty is to avoid **conflict**.

CHECKPOINT: WHAT WOULD YOU DO?

You had a late night at karate practice and were too tired to do your math homework when you got home. You went to bed knowing it was not done. The next morning, your teacher asks the class to hand in their homework. You tell your teacher that you forgot to do it.

Were you being truthful or dishonest?
Can you explain why?

WHY DO WE LIE?

Can you remember the last time you told a lie?

Why did you do it? How did it make you feel?

Believe it or not, lying is a normal part of being a kid. You may want to avoid getting in trouble, or maybe you're too embarrassed to share what really happened. Whatever the reason, being dishonest often leads to feeling guilty about misleading someone. This feeling is called **remorse**. When we feel remorse, we feel bad about being dishonest.

EMOTIONS AND LYING

Our **emotions** can sometimes lead us to lie or say something that we know is not true.

We may lie because we feel ashamed.

We may lie because we feel embarrassed.

We may lie because we are fearful of a consequence.

You may be too ashamed or embarrassed to tell your teacher the truth about why you did not do your math homework. You may even be afraid that she will take away your recess.

No matter what the emotion is, being honest about your mistakes will make you feel better than lying.

DID YOU KNOW?

Emotions are usually the biggest factors that shape our behaviors.

UNDERSTANDING INTEGRITY

When you choose to be honest, you are showing that you have integrity.

The word integrity means that you do the right thing, even when no one is watching.

It's easy to be dishonest when you feel ashamed, embarrassed, or fearful. Making the choice to tell the truth, even if it leads to a negative consequence, shows that you have integrity.

Telling your teacher the truth about why you did not do your math homework shows that you have integrity.

DID YOU KNOW?

Sometimes being honest requires bravery.

UNDERSTANDING RESPONSIBILITY

A big part of telling the truth depends on your sense of responsibility.

Being responsible means that you understand what is expected of you, and that you work hard to meet those expectations. It also means if you don't meet them, you are honest about it, and try again to succeed.

Telling your teacher the truth about why you did not do your math homework and offering to make it up shows that you have a sense of responsibility towards your homework.

CHECKPOINT: WHAT WOULD YOU DO?

Your teacher believes you when you say you forgot to do your math homework. You realize, though, that this is dishonest because you did not forget. Instead, you chose not to do it because you were too tired from karate practice. You want your teacher to trust you and you want to be honest with her.

What would you tell your teacher?

HONESTY

DID YOU KNOW?

Being honest about something you did wrong means you want to understand what you should have done right.

UNDERSTANDING ACCOUNTABILITY

Another big part of telling the truth depends on your sense of accountability.

The word accountability means that you accept responsibility for something. If you had a responsibility to do your math homework, but chose not to because you were too tired from karate practice, you show accountability by telling your teacher the truth about why your homework is not done.

Telling your teacher that it was your decision not to do your homework, instead of pretending that you forgot, shows accountability.

DID YOU KNOW?

Honesty means more than not lying. It means your actions are true too.

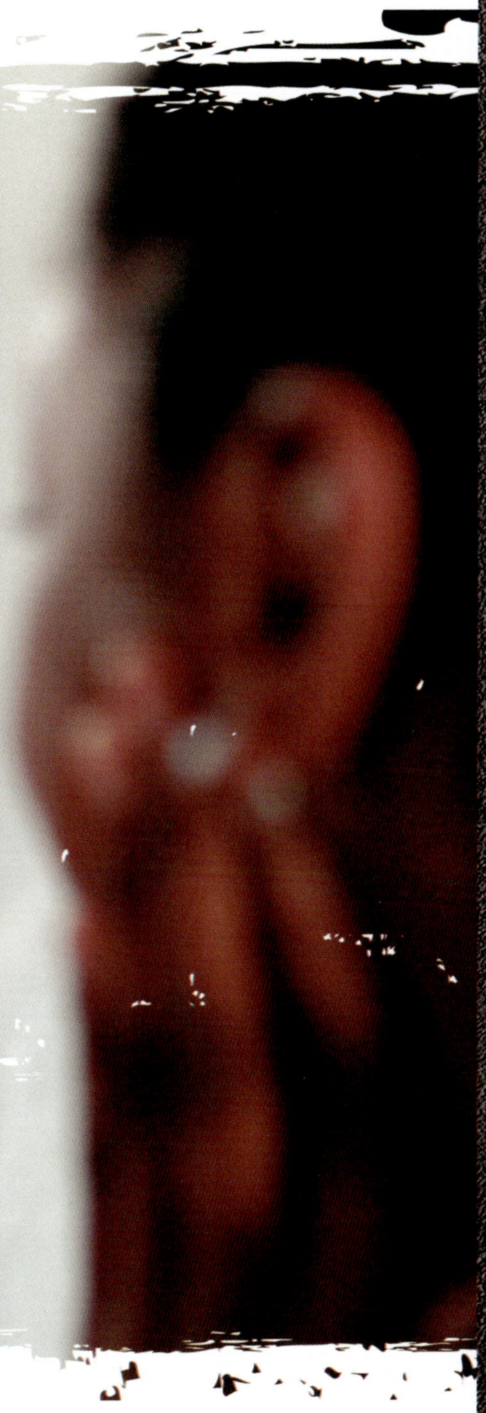

HOW TO FIX A LIE

Although we cannot take back the things we say, we can try to fix them, or make things better. Ever wondered how to fix a lie?

You may have been dishonest and lied to your teacher when you told her you forgot to do your math homework. But this lie can be fixed!

You can demonstrate integrity by telling the truth, responsibility by offering to make up the work, and accountability by taking the blame. This is what's called a **teachable moment**, or a mistake that you can learn from.

LEARNING TO BE HONEST

Being honest and telling the truth is not always easy. But it's worth it!

Everyone makes mistakes. But seeing mistakes as teachable moments helps us learn more about ourselves. We may tell a lie, but later feel remorse. This could lead to a breakthrough in your sense of integrity, responsibility, and accountability—the choice is yours!

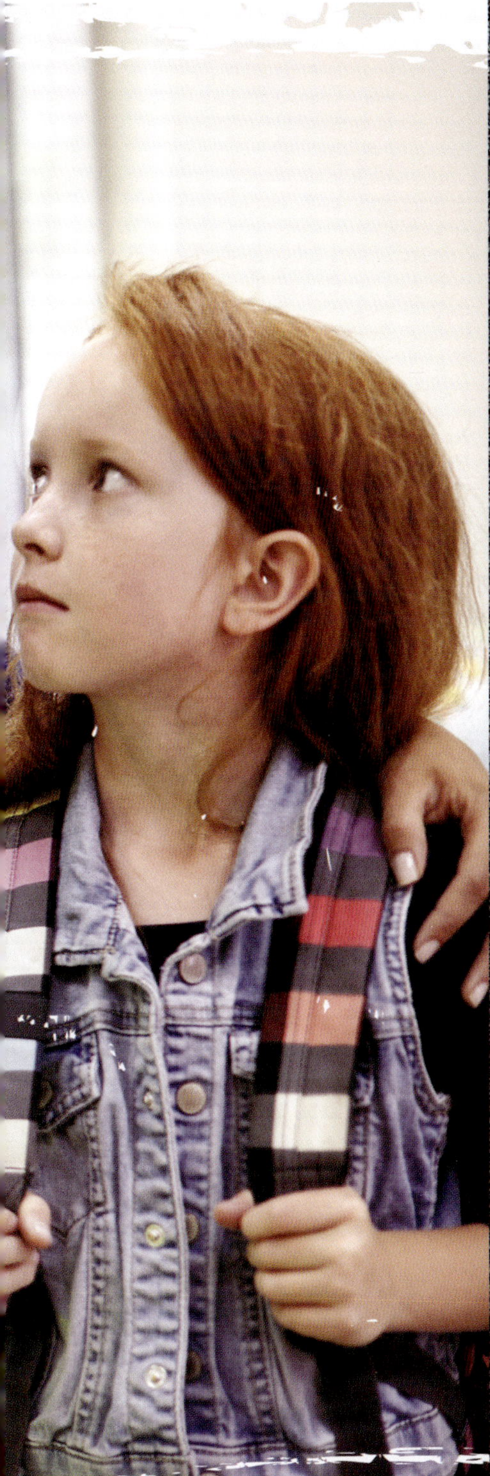

A BETTER YOU

Let's revisit the last example.

Now, what would you tell your teacher when she asks for your math homework?

How would you demonstrate integrity, responsibility, and accountability?

What did you learn from your teachable moment?

GLOSSARY

accountability (uh·kown·tuh·BIL·i·tee): Taking credit or blame for your own actions

conflict (KON·flikt): A strong disagreement or argument

emotions (ih·MOH·shunz): Strong feelings, such as fear, anger, or joy

honest (ON·ist): Truthful

integrity (in·TEH·gruh·tee): The quality of being honest and doing the right thing

remorse (ruh·MORS): A feeling of being sorry for doing something wrong

responsibility (ruh·spaan·suh·BIL·uh·tee): A willingness to answer for your own actions

self-esteem (SELF eh·STEEM): A feeling of having respect for yourself

teachable moment (TEE·chuh·buhl MOW·muhnt): An event or experience that provides an opportunity to learn something new

truth (TROOTH): The real facts about something

INDEX

accountability 6, 23, 25, 29

ashamed 14, 16

consequence 14, 16

dishonesty 8, 10, 12, 16, 20, 25

emotion 14

honesty 6, 7, 8, 14, 16, 17, 18, 20, 22, 24

integrity 6, 16, 25, 27, 29

lie 12, 14, 25, 27

remorse 12, 27

self-esteem 7

WEBSITES TO VISIT

edutopia.org/blog/film-festival-kindness-empathy-connection

safeshare.tv/x/ss5bb2267004e1c# (a fable about honesty)

https://pbskids.org/arthur/friends/francines-tough-day

ABOUT THE AUTHOR

Vicky Bureau was born in Longueuil, Quebec, and was raised in South Florida. As a teacher, she developed a passion for the social and emotional growth of her students, and later transitioned into the area of child and adolescent psychology after earning her master's degree in school counseling. In addition to working with children, Vicky loves to be surrounded by animals and nature. She lives in Fort Lauderdale with her family: Billy, Khloe, M.J., and Max; her three cats, Alley, Baguette, and Salem; and her dog, Boomer.

Written by: Vicky Bureau
Designed by: Rhea Magaro Wallace
Interior designed by: Kathy Walsh
Series Development: James Earley
Proofreader: Melissa Boyce
Educational Consultant: Marie Lemke M.Ed.

Photographs: Shutterstock Cover robert_s, Viktoriia Protsak, Tom Wang; Background robert_s; Color Splash Viktoriia Protsak, Box p 7, 9, 15, 17, 22, 24 Puwadol Jaturawutthichai; p 5 Dean Drobot; p 7 Rawpixel.com; p 9 BlurryMe; p 10 Jason Richeux; p 11 DGLimages; p 13 Asier Romero; p 15 CREATISTA; p 17 New Africa; p 19 VH-studio; p 21 Ollyy; p 22 Ground Picture; p 24 True Touch Lifestyle; p 26 Pressmaster; p 28 gpointstudio

Crabtree Publishing

crabtreebooks.com 800-387-7650

Printed in the U.S.A./012023/CG20220815

Published in Canada
Crabtree Publishing
616 Welland Ave.
St. Catharines, Ontario
L2M 5V6

Published in the United States
Crabtree Publishing
347 Fifth Ave
Suite 1402-145
New York, NY 10016

Library and Archives Canada Cataloguing in Publication
Available at Library and Archives Canada

Library of Congress Cataloging-in-Publication Data
Available at the Library of Congress

Hardcover: 978-1-0396-6047-2
Paperback: 978-1-0396-6242-1
Ebook (pdf): 978-1-0396-7038-9
Epub: 978-1-0396-7236-9